THE WORLD'S SHORTEST BOOK ON RELATIONSHIPS

THE WORLD'S SHORTEST BOOK ON RELATIONSHIPS

Discover the ONLY Reason Relationships Fail

BY LARRY DANIELS SR

DEDICATION

I dedicate this book to all the beautiful relationships I've destroyed due to my own ignorance on the subject.

TABLE OF CONTENTS

MY GOAL AND DESIRE

I'm very impatient when it comes to learning. I want to know now. I'm sick of long, drawn-out presentations where the person is speaking while someone is drawing for 20 minutes. Then, when you are about to get into the subject matter promised, the speaker says, "But first, let me tell you about myself." ARGH!

30 more minutes.

This book doesn't drag things out. I've attempted to make this work short, powerful and useable without a lot of fluff.

Please acknowledge my desire to empower couples, those considering becoming couples and those who have given up on trying to be a part of a couple.

I ask that you do not copy this book, which is very easy to do given the number of pages, because that wouldn't help me financially. I am sincerely trying to help individuals who are trying to become more competent in creating relationships, because competent individuals create competent couples, competent couples make society better and a competent society is full of happier people. One pillar of happiness is integrity, so I trust you'll have integrity and insist that anyone interested in this subject purchase their own copy to further enable me to continue working, making this world a happier, improved planet, which is what I promised my children when I decided to bring them into this world.

In other words, please don't cheat me and my family by making free copies.

LET'S GET TO IT!!!!

"WHAT'S YOUR PROBLEM?"

You can't have trouble with something you understand. So, let's gain some understanding.

A problem is something that goes against your desire(s).

How do we create problems? By looking at a given situation and deciding we don't like it.

How do we solve problems? By placing our attention on a situation and raising our intelligence on the subject, we can affect the problem to our desired outcome.

Who is the problem creator in your life? You are.

Who is the problem solver in your life? Right again! You are, although you may not be a good one…yet.

I could take a look at something such as drunk driving and have a strong desire to find a solution for the number of deaths it causes.

Someone else might look at the same situation and never give it another thought.

With this understanding, I'd ask, who does every problem in the world belong to? Yes. You! You created it by agreeing that it's wrong or improper, etc. You can solve your problems (if you know how). You can ignore them or just continue to complain.

There are only 2 reasons a problem doesn't get corrected:

1. The person in charge of the problem doesn't know how to fix it (ignorance).

OR

2. The person in charge just isn't fixing it (lazy or has another agenda).

If you want to discover why things continue in a certain way, find out who is in charge of the area and if they don't know what to do or if they're just not doing their job. Both reasons can be handled if the person in charge has a genuine desire to be responsible for the problem.

This next exercise, which is the main component of this work, is designed for you to have a good, honest look at what you do or do not understand about relationships.

Please sit down with your partner, friends, or a learning group; this would also be very beneficial to teenagers on the brink of dating. Ensure that each person has their own copy of this work and, without using a dictionary or any device other than your mind, define the following words. Don't discuss anything until everyone has completed the exercise. Then, discuss what you've discovered about your relationship vocabulary.

These discussions will help orient those participating in relationship culture. We all need to be properly oriented and educated about relationships if we're ever going to break the cycle of divorce and one-parent homes that plague us currently. You can take things into your own hands or allow television and social media to teach your children how to interact with their romantic partners.

HAVE FUN!!!!

"WHAT DO YOU MEAN?"

P lease, review the following list of words and honestly grade yourself on your knowledge of relationship terminology.

Write your definition in the space provided. Do not cheat by using a dictionary or asking others for their definition. Relying on others to clarify your life is a major problem in relationships. We will clear up the words later. Use this as a self-assessment to grade any progress you might make as a result of reading this book. Once your definition has been made, leave it alone. Most importantly, have fun learning.

- **Affection**
- **Fond**
- **Love**
- **Partnership**
- **Trust**
- **Integrity**
- **Honesty**
- **Dedication**
- **Husband**
- **Steward**
- **Wife**

- **Marriage**
- **Responsible**
- **Success**
- **Right**
- **Wrong**
- **Happy**
- **Good**
- **Bad**
- **Goal**
- **Relationship**
- **Boyfriend**
- **Girlfriend**
- **Doubt**
- **Favored**
- **Communication**
- **Exchange**
- **Sex**
- **Children**
- **Parent**
- **Subordinate**
- **Role**
- **Create**
- **Artistic**
- **Art**
- **Aesthetic**
- **Beauty**
- **Truth**
- **Sincere**
- **Cause**
- **Effect**
- **Game**
- **Amuse**
- **Fun**
- **Content**
- **Satisfy**
- **Gratify**

- **Conditioned**
- **Problem**
- **Friend**
- **Control**
- **Independent**
- **Support**
- **Fail**
- **Money**
- **Together**
- **Master**
- **Struggle**
- **Vigorous**
- **Man**
- **Woman**
- **Need**
- **Necessary**
- **Want**
- **Deserve**
- **King**
- **Queen**
- **Preeminent**
- **Submissive**
- **Docile**
- **Player**
- **Team**
- **We**
- **Union**
- **A**
- **Part**
- **Apart**

Did you realize anything from the words you defined or couldn't define? I would bet there is a correlation between the number of undefined or incorrectly defined words and the difficulties one finds in his/her relationships.

WHAT I MEAN

I hope the previous exercise was enlightening (it certainly was for me) and fun. Some words have many meanings. The following list that I have comprised is not the "right" definition by any means. Instead, it is my personal list. That is what I mean when I use these words in relation to relationships. Remember, I am not trying to change your mind about anything. I only want to share the information which has brought me some relief in my life. Clarifying what you mean will clear up what you want for yourself. Defining what you mean is vital in any life activity, especially relationships. Once you are certain about what you desire and can explain it to a potential husband/wife or boyfriend /girlfriend, they are free to accept the position of life partner or look elsewhere for a better opportunity. Please read "What I mean" so that we may have a starting ground from which we can work and begin to discuss how we want to create our lives.

Affection: A fond or tender feeling toward another.

Fond: A strong liking.

Love: An expression of one's affection.

Partnership: A person associated with another in a common activity or interest.

Trust: Total confidence in the integrity, ability and good character of another.

Integrity: The quality of being undivided; completeness; ability to say what you see.

Honesty: The quality of being sincere, not deceptive.

Dedication: The act of committing (ones' self) to a particular course of thought or action.

Husband: A manager or steward of a house; the master of a house.

Steward: One who manages another's property, finances, or other affairs.

Wife: A married woman.

Marriage: A close union; legal union of a man and a woman as husband and wife (please note there is no mention of love in most dictionaries).

Responsible: Capable of being trusted and depended on; one who causes things willingly.

Success: The gaining of something desired, planned, or attempted.

Right: Appropriate, moral, something which causes or creates more survival than destruction.

Wrong: Not in conformity with truth; unfair or unjust; inappropriate; something that creates more destruction than survival.

Happy: Cheerful, not worried.

Good: Of moral excellence; promoting survival.

Bad: Not reaching an adequate standard; not functioning properly; Non-survival.

Goal: The objective toward which an endeavor is directed.

Relationship: The state or fact of being connected.

Boyfriend: A favored male companion.

Girlfriend: A favored female companion.

Favored: Treated, looked upon with special kindness or liking.

Doubt: To tend to distrust; disbelieve.

Communication: The exchange of ideas with intention, attention, understanding and acknowledgment.

Exchange: To give up one thing for another; to take or give in return for something else.

Sex/Intercourse: Exchange or communications between persons, usually physical in nature.

Children: The descendants of men and women who will project the race into the future and create society.

Parent: An ancestor, guardian, or protector; an entity in a hierarchical structure to which other entities are subordinate.

Subordinate: Belonging to a class or rank lower than another. Subject to the control or authority of another.

Create: To bring into existence; to produce through artistic or imaginative effort.

Artistic: One who performs one's work as if it were an art.

Art: Conscious arrangement or production of sounds (words), movements, colors, forms, or other elements in a way that affects the aesthetic sense.

Aesthetic: Of or relating to beauty.

Beauty: A pleasing quality associated with truthfulness.

Truth: Sincere.

Sincere: Presenting no false appearance.

Cause: A person or thing that produces an effect, result, or consequence.

Effect: Something brought about by a cause.

Game: A way of amusing oneself.

Amuse: To cause, to laugh, or smile by giving pleasure.

Fun: A source of enjoyment or pleasure.

Content: Satisfied.

Satisfy: To gratify the need, desire, or expectation of; to be free from doubt or question.

Gratify: To give what is desired.

Conditioned: Prepared for a specific action or process.

Process: A series of actions or steps towards achieving a particular end.

Problem: A situation that presents something that is different from what is desired, which confuses one or causes one to lose his bearings; counter intention.

Confusion: The state of being uncertain or bewildered; a state of disorder; mistaking of one person or thing for another; random motion.

Friend: A person with whom one is allied in a struggle or cause.

Struggle: To be vigorously involved with a task or undertaking, making forceful efforts to get free.

Vigorous: Lively.

Free: Not or no longer confined, obstructed, or fixed (free to do what).

Control: To start, change, or stop something or someone.

Independent: Free from the influence, guidance, or control of another or others.

Support: To keep from failing.

Fail: To prove so deficient as to be totally ineffective; to be unsuccessful.

Effective: Producing a desired or intended result.

Money: A medium that can be exchanged for goods and services; a form of energy that creates options.

Energy: The strength and vitality required for sustained activity.

Together: In harmony.

Harmony: The quality of forming a pleasing and consistent whole.

Whole: A thing that is complete in itself.

Master: One with control over the action of another or others; adjective, which means having great skill or proficiency.

Man: An adult male who is responsible for himself and others (if necessary).

Woman: An adult female who is responsible for herself and others (if necessary).

Need: A lack of something necessary.

Necessary: Absolutely required. Indispensable.

Want: To wish for; to be lacking; request; desire.

Deserve: To be worthy of; to serve zealously (the root word is serve).

Serve: Perform duties or services for; treat in a specified way; be of use in fulfilling (a purpose).

King: The most powerful or eminent of a group or place.

Power: The capacity to influence other people or the course of events; a right or authority given or delegated to a person or body.

Eminent: Respected; distinguished.

Queen: A woman regarded as preeminent in a domain.

Regard: Think of in a certain way.

Pre-eminent: Superior to or notable above all others.

Superior: Higher in status, quality, or power; of high standard or quality.

All: Any whatever.

Think: Direct one's mind towards someone or something; use one's mind actively to form connected ideas.

Submissive: Docile.

Docile: Easily instructed; teachable.

Player: One who participates in a game; who performs a role.

Role: The characteristic and social behavior expected of an individual; position or function.

Team: A group organized to work together.

Organized: Order.

Order: A state in which everything is in its correct place.

Work: Activity involving mental or physical effort, done in order to achieve a result.

Perfect: Without flaw.

Flaw: An imperfection.

We: Used instead of I.

A: One.

Part: A piece combined with others to make up a whole; a person's contribution to an action or situation.

Apart: Into pieces.

Feel free to adopt any of these meanings for yourself or to disregard any that you don't agree with. But, most importantly, have definitions for yourself and make sure you can explain them to a potential partner. If you cannot explain the definitions clearly, you do not have an understanding of what you want. Your partner must be able to do the same for: "How can two walk together lest they are agreed?" Amos 3:3.

Clarifying the role you expect to play and, more importantly, the role you expect another to play, is vital to a successful relationship. Imagine hiring someone to manage your business or work for you and not satisfactorily explaining their job description, responsibilities and duties: you expect them to open the doors at 9 am and they don't show up until 11 am; payday is Friday, but the manager doesn't cut the checks until Monday. This could be disastrous.

Disastrous: Highly Unsuccessful.

The most recent census data states that 39% of marriages end in divorce, with the number one stated reason being money problems. Hmm, imagine if pre-couples would define *good income*, *budget*, *what percent of our salary will be saved,* and *financial goals* **BEFORE** getting married?

People cannot do what they cannot define. If you ever notice someone having difficulty **PERFORMING** a task, ask them to define the words associated with that task. I think you'll be amazed.

If a surgeon's assistant never defined a scalpel, he couldn't pass one to a surgeon.

If a man and woman never agreed upon the definition of a husband and wife, it is doubtful they could create a stable, happy, productive, secure relationship.

"THE ONLY CAUSE OF RELATIONSHIP FAILURE"

Often, when I tell people there's only one reason for relationship failure, they ask, "What is it?" When I explain the answer, they usually say, "Well, that's obvious."

Is it? If one saw an obvious train coming directly at him, if one were sane, he would get out of the way. If the cause were obvious, separations wouldn't be so high. Why don't we take the obvious and control it when things begin to go downhill? The issue, at least from my perspective, is this: a romantic relationship isn't natural.

While it's perfectly natural to be attracted to others, desire for affection and companionship is natural, the act of dedicating oneself to another for a lifetime certainly is not natural.

Once an egg is fertilized, there's nothing left to do except keep the woman alive. Let nature take its' course. It's natural.

However, when two human beings decide to become a couple, the decision requires a constant supply of energy and effort for the relationship to be considered viable.

From the time of the agreement until the relationship ends (and it will end either due to death or mutual agreement), it must be constantly fed energy from both partners, just like a campfire must be fed wood. Every moment the relationship exists, the participants must constantly find a reason to want to enhance or improve the other person's life. This energy is non-negotiable. Not every day, but every moment.

The purpose of having a relationship, in my perspective, is to enhance one another's lives as you share in the day-to-day experiences of living. Giving your attention and energy (financial, sexual, physical, emotional, etc.) to your partner constantly, as their needs dictate, is the bond that'll ensure the success of the union. Forsaking others and making that person know that they are your priority is what separates single people from couples. However, it's not natural. It is a moral agreement. This seems to be mainly a human phenomenon. Only a few examples exist in nature of lifelong mates. Most mammals mate and then go their separate ways until mating season rolls around again. *Hey, handsome, thank you very much. See ya!*

These agreements must be created by the personal motivations of the people involved.

AND WHEN ONE OR BOTH PEOPLE IN THE RELATIONSHIP STOP CREATING IT, IT CEASES TO EXIST. IT ENDS!

That's the one reason relationships end, the creators of it (for whatever reason) do not continue to create it.

When one doesn't give his/her energy freely and cheerfully the relationship begins to decline. It takes two people giving their all to cause a relationship. There will be ups and downs for certain, but like a Navy seal, if you quit, you're outta here. You lose all the rights and privileges of maintaining the title called: partner.

"PUTTING DEFINITIONS INTO PERSPECTIVE"

As we've already covered for a relationship to exist it must be created.

(Bring into existence through artistic or imaginative effort)

Artistic: Of or pertaining to art or artists.

Art: Something considered beautiful.

Artist: One who consciously arranges colors, shapes, objects, sounds, or things to create art.

When you were dating, did you arrange things consciously? Were your clothes ironed, makeup (colors), shapes (haircut, nails trimmed), sounds (spoke in a sweet and kind manner)?

Imaginative: Dealing with your imagination. What ideas do you have when you're imagining your relationship? Caring for one another, compassion, love, or violence, frustration, stress and anger?

How do you bring forth the ideas in your mind for the world to see? Are you actively involved in creating those ideas or do you just let things happen?

Effort: Work.

Work deals with moving things. In this case, we are attempting to move the romantic ideas in your mind into the real world by consciously arranging colors, shapes, sounds, objects, etc., like an artist would create something beautiful.

Beauty generally deals with symmetry, which means things are evenly placed or equal. We rarely agree that a person with one large eye up high and one small eye near his cheek is beautiful. How about a woman with one large breast and one small one? These ideas are subjective and deal with physicality. However, we are trying to get to the understanding that what must be symmetrical or properly aligned are your thoughts about what a good relationship is and your creative actions. Do your relationship thoughts align with your relationship actions?

The subject here is you, not your partner and if he or she deserves to be treated in a certain way. Your thoughts and actions are the topic. You are the manager of your creations. So, if your life doesn't reflect the mental images you desire, perhaps you need to get busy consciously arranging things to create whatever you think a beautiful relationship is.

"THERE'S NOTHING WRONG WITH YOUR PARTNER"

Again, feel free to disagree, but this is my perspective. To reiterate, relationships aren't natural and must be created by the two, causing them to exist.

Husband: From Old Norse Husband; manager or steward of a home.

Manager: One who sees the daily operations of a business or institution.

Steward: One who has control over the activities, finances and affairs of another.

A man is said to be the King of his castle (home) and supported by his queen.

King: A man considered eminent (most powerful) in a given area; no other male has more authority than a king.

Queen: Woman considered pre-eminent in a realm.

This had me thinking: if the man is eminent, how can the woman be pre-eminent? In my mind, men are generally the aggressors in initiating relationships, but the relationship isn't official (traditionally) until the woman gives the green light. If the man tries to proceed without her permission, it is usually considered a felony. In this regard, she comes first in the union, because it doesn't exist until she accepts.

So, the man applies for the job of being a husband (which is the manager of a household) and the woman agrees. She just hired (gave permission) someone to manage her affairs, control her activities and finances.

Well, if we were to view relationships as businesses and he is the manager, who is the owner?

Exactly, the queen! Would you hire a manager for your business and then attempt to do all the work? No. The owner of the business supports their manager, giving him the resources needed, so that he can stay strong and run her business. The more he accomplishes for the business, the more she will have for herself.

If your business is screwed up, who the hell hired the incompetent manager?

Don't be in a rush to fire your manager, maybe he just needs some training or something to energize or motivate him. Sweet gentle counsel, a home cooked meal, some praise, or intimacy may be a few items needed to get him working for you. That way, you can enjoy the rewards of a relationship that was beautifully arranged consciously.

Some things are required, however, to run a business together. Similar goals and desires for the same things. You must be close in intelligence and both must have a similar understanding of communication.

When professional musicians (musical artists) get together, they must be in time and harmony to make music. They generally have a different skill set concerning an arrangement of sound than a grade school musician. A professional demonstrates this understanding when he performs. A child playing an instrument in grade school may not have the same skillset and, therefore, makes sounds and attempts to create music, but the understanding or experience may not be present. Although they are both musicians, they do not have the same understanding and skills.

If partners aren't in harmony, they cannot make music and will just make noise.

There's nothing wrong with your partner. Perhaps the two of you just aren't on the same sheet of music. Stop blaming one another for playing a different song and work on your ability to be in harmony with each other.

"CREATE YOUR RELATIONSHIP"

Your relationship is already perfect! It is without any imperfections, because it is exactly what you (both of you) have created.

Let me explain: understand that if you take a hammer and hit a wooden table with it, the mark left on the table is perfect; It is without flaw. So, when I speak of perfection, I am speaking about effect from actions. Please do not confuse this concept with our desires or wants. To further make my point, I am a trained marksman, and every time I go to the range, it is my desire to score 100%, which I do quite frequently. However, whenever I have a shot group that is spread out a little further than I want it to be, I look at the target and know that my creation is perfect, meaning a flawless reflection of my aim and trigger squeeze. There has never been a time when I hit the target and there was no bullet hole in the exact spot where my round impacted. Nor have I ever missed the target and had a hole magically appear. My targets (creations) were always perfect, meaning the exact reflection of what I have done.

Please do not confuse the concept of perfection with the concept of success. Being successful means getting your desired result. If you want romance and have romance, you're successful in romance. If you like to be verbally abused and your partner degrades you on a megaphone in front of the largest crowd publicly available whenever they feel upset - congratulations, you too are successful. If you love watching your children cry whenever they hear the adults in the house scream at the tops of their voices and you get to see this periodically - once again, success.

If you do not like to have sex, and you have a woman who constantly attempts to make love to you, you have an unsuccessful love life, although you may make love seven times a week. If we understand and agree to the definitions of success and perfect, we could make the statement that everyone has a perfect relationship. That agreement would place us in the fantastic position of being responsible for the situations we find ourselves in. It would also get us to stop blaming others for our misery and begin to redefine what is acceptable to us and what is not. Once this dialogue takes place between potential lovers, I hope more successful relationships will begin to blossom and lower the divorce rate we are currently experiencing.

"CREATION EXERCISE"

Now that we have a point from which to start, I'd like you to begin an exercise:

Close your eyes and dream about your successful relationship. I want you to take as much time as you need and create whatever you want. There is no limit (except what you place on yourself) to your perfect picture. You have carte blanch. Think about where you live, how you spend your days, how you and your mate interact with yourselves and others, including children. Do you frequent parties or do you spend a lot of time together intimately? Do you laugh often? Do you feel special? How is your sex life? Does it make the little hairs on the back of your neck stand up just thinking about him or her touching you? Create! Create! Create! Once you are satisfied that you have successfully fantasized and developed an idea in your mind about the type of life you want for yourself and your partner, open your eyes and begin to consciously arrange colors, shapes, sounds and objects to make those ideas a reality. Have fun. No one is watching.

Wasn't that fun?

There is no reason you cannot enjoy all, most, or some of the things you just created in your mind. As we cleared the word earlier, to create something is to take an idea or thought from your mind and bring it into reality.

"CONCLUSION"

THANK YOU for reading, I truly hope you've taken something from this work and can use it to better your life.

Please support me and my goal to create more competent couples in this world.

Word of mouth is a great advertisement. You could also purchase copies and give them away to friends and family. Knowledge is power!

More happy couples will help raise the tone of society, and one day, with enough happy people, we will know world peace. When individuals become competent, they no longer feel helpless in the area of life called ability. So, the more people there are who realize the one thing that causes relationships to fail, the more people there will be who can avoid the trap and create a successful relationship. So, let's get more (paid) copies into circulation so more people can get busy consciously arranging colors, shapes, objects and sounds, just like artists do. Then, they will enjoy the beautiful experiences life offers to competent couples.

All the best,

LARRY DANIELS SR.

A Short Story To Remind You That...

"LOVE IS A VERB"

I picked this story up somewhere along this life's journey and do not recall the source. It's such a clear example of love I had to share it with you.

When a couple dies and goes to heaven, they are mandated to sit across from one another for breakfast, lunch and dinner. The food is catered by God himself; therefore, everything is always perfectly cooked, ripe and prepared impeccably. The only issue is the couple has long extensions placed on their hands, so it's impossible for a person to feed himself. So, the arrangement is the lovers must feed one another to enjoy the beautiful meals God has prepared for them.

When a couple dies and goes to hell, they, too, are mandated to sit across from one another with the same food catered by the same God and attached to the same extensions. However, the couples in hell are in extreme agony, because they are starving to death. See, the people in hell just refuse to feed one another.

I was told this repeatedly by my friend's mother when I was a teenager…

"LOVE DON'T HURT!"

Ms. Mary

It is very possible to have a happy, stable relationship... when you know how. This short book was created to remove all doubt concerning why relationships fail. Once you understand the sole cause of breakups, you can navigate toward the romantic destination you desire. Together, we can create a healthy society, one couple at a time.

All the Best,
Larry.

theonlyreasonrelationshipsfail@gmail.com